W9-CGZ-385

WITHDRAWN

Extreme Dinosaurs!

Smithsonian | Collins
An Imprint of HarperCollinsPublishers

Q&A

Smithsonian Mission Statement

For more than 160 years, the Smithsonian has remained true to its mission, "the increase and diffusion of knowledge." Today the Smithsonian is not only the world's largest provider of museum experiences supported by authoritative scholarship in science, history, and the arts but also an international leader in scientific research and exploration. The Smithsonian offers the world a picture of America, and America a picture of the world.

Special thanks to Dr. Matthew Carrano, curator, National Museum of Natural History, Smithsonian Institution, for his invaluable contribution to this book.

This book was created by **jacob packaged goods** LLC (www.jpgglobal.com)
Written by: Sarah L. Thomson
Creative: Ellen Jacob, Jeff Chandler, Carolyn Jackson, Andrea Curley

Illustrations, unless listed below: © Karen Carr

Other credits: **cover (inset), pages 6, 7, 23 (inset), 25, 27, 40:** © François Gohier/Photo Researchers, Inc.; **page 8:** © Richard T. Nowitz/Photo Researchers, Inc.; **page 9:** © Ted Kinsman/Photo Researchers, Inc.; **pages 20–21:** © Chase Studio/Photo Researchers, Inc.; **page 23:** © Chris Butler/Photo Researchers, Inc.; **page 38:** © Randall B. Henne/Dembinsky Photo Assoc.; **page 39:** © Joseph Nettis/Photo Researchers, Inc.; **page 45:** top: © Chip Clark; bottom: Scott Sampson, National Museum of Natural History.

Contents

Some had scales. Some had feathers. Some munched leaves and twigs. Some hunted down other animals and ate their flesh. But they were all dinosaurs. They all had some things in common.

Dinosaurs lived on dry land, not in oceans, rivers, or lakes. Their babies hatched out of eggs, as birds and reptiles do today. They walked with their legs straight under their bodies, not out sideways like a crocodile's or a lizard's legs.

And all dinosaurs lived between 230 and 65 million years ago—long before there were people on Earth.

Archaeopteryx was an early kind of bird that lived when dinosaurs did.

SMITHSONIAN LINK
The next time you visit Washington, DC, don't forget to pay a visit to the amazing Dinosaur Hall at the National Museum of Natural History: http://photo2.si.edu/dino/dino.html

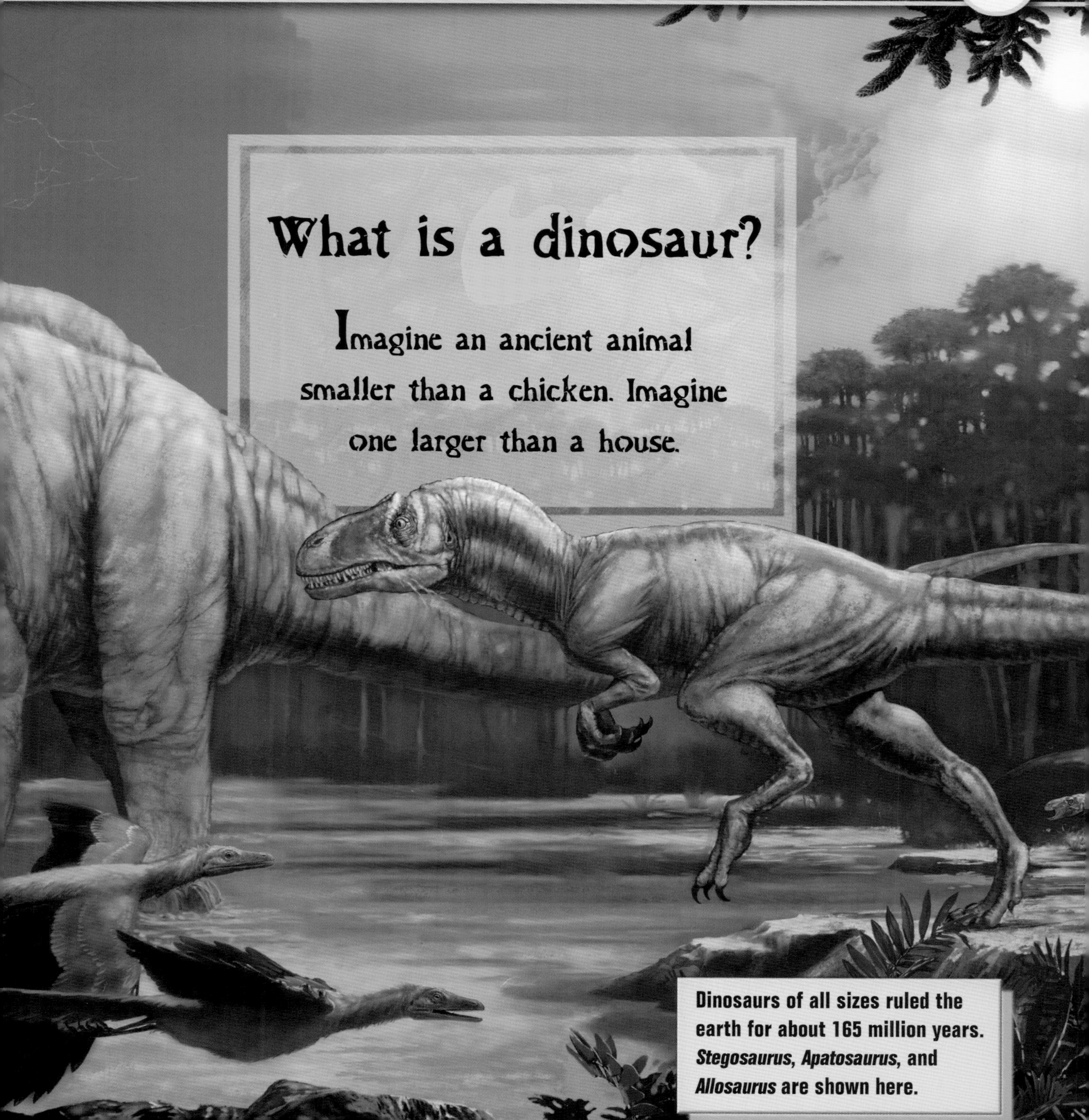

What is a dinosaur?

Imagine an ancient animal smaller than a chicken. Imagine one larger than a house.

Dinosaurs of all sizes ruled the earth for about 165 million years. *Stegosaurus*, *Apatosaurus*, and *Allosaurus* are shown here.

If dinosaurs lived long ago, how do we know about them?

Dinosaurs died out millions of years ago. But they left something behind—**fossils**.

Here is one way a dinosaur could become a fossil:

1. A dinosaur dies.
2. Its body is buried in sand or mud.
3. The soft parts of the body rot away. Only bones and teeth are left.
4. Water in the ground seeps into tiny holes in the bones and teeth. The water has **minerals** dissolved in it.
5. The water dissolves away the original bone bit by bit, leaving the minerals in its place. What's left is a fossil, an exact stone copy of the dinosaur's skeleton.

Did every dinosaur become a fossil?

Most dinosaurs never turned into fossils. After they died, their bodies were eaten and their bones rotted. The few that did become fossils lay underground for millions of years before they were discovered.

Not only dinosaurs turned into fossils. Other animals did, too, like this trilobite, a small ocean-dwelling creature.

SMITHSONIAN LINK
Paleontologists know many tricks for hunting fossils.
Go on a virtual dinosaur dig and hunt for yourself:
http://www.nmnh.si.edu/paleo/dinosaurs/interactives/dig/main.html

Most of the time paleontologists find only a few fossilized bones. It is rare to find a complete skeleton.

Who hunts for fossils?

A scientist who studies ancient life by examining fossils is called a **paleontologist**. One of the things paleontologists do is hunt for fossils.

They start by looking for rock that was sand or mud when dinosaurs lived. Over time that sand or mud changed to rock—rock that might have dinosaur fossils in it. Paleontologists check for small fossils on the ground or for bits of bigger fossils poking up through the rock. If they find some, they start to dig.

Paleontologists hope they might discover an entire skeleton. They can put that skeleton back together bone by bone, and we can see what a live dinosaur might have looked like.

> Paleontologists use special tools to dig up dinosaur fossils. These include a rock hammer, trowel, paintbrush (to remove dust), an ice pick, awls, a cement trowel, and a whisk broom.

paleontologist:
PAY-lee-on-TAHL-uh-jist

SMITHSONIAN LINK

At the National Museum of Natural History, you can watch experts extracting fossils from rocks at the Vertebrate Paleo Prep Lab. Not going to Washington, DC, in the near future? That's okay—you can experience the Paleo Prep Lab through an interactive, online slide show!
http://www.nmnh.si.edu/paleo/dinosaurs/collection/labs/vpLab/index.html

Triassic

Jurassic

Cretaceous

What was the dinosaurs' world like?

It's one thing to see a dinosaur's skeleton. It's another to imagine that dinosaur alive. What was it like during the time of the dinosaurs?

For most of that time, the world was probably hotter. Some land that is dry today was covered by shallow seas, and there were no **ice caps** at the North and South Poles.

Dinosaurs lived during the Mesozoic era—which is broken down into three parts: the Triassic, Jurassic, and Cretaceous periods.

When dinosaurs first appeared in the Triassic, there were giant ferns and trees with needles (like pine trees today). Later, plants with flowers first bloomed. Small, furry **mammals** hid in trees and burrows. Crocodiles swam in the rivers. Cockroaches scurried under rocks.

But not all the animals soaring through the sky were birds.

Quetzalcoatlus

Could dinosaurs fly?

Flying **reptiles** called pterosaurs lived at the same time as dinosaurs. Their wings were covered with stretched skin, not feathered like birds' wings.

Some pterosaurs were so tiny, they could have sat in your hands. Others were huge. *Quetzalcoatlus* had wings as wide as a small plane's.

No flying creature has ever been bigger.

Pterosaurs looked a bit like dinosaurs, but they were a different kind of animal.

Were there any dinosaurs that flew? Some small, feathered dinosaurs may have hopped off the ground to catch their food or jumped from tree branches to the earth. Over millions of years, their bodies developed the muscles and bones they needed to fly. These dinosaurs gave rise to modern-day birds.

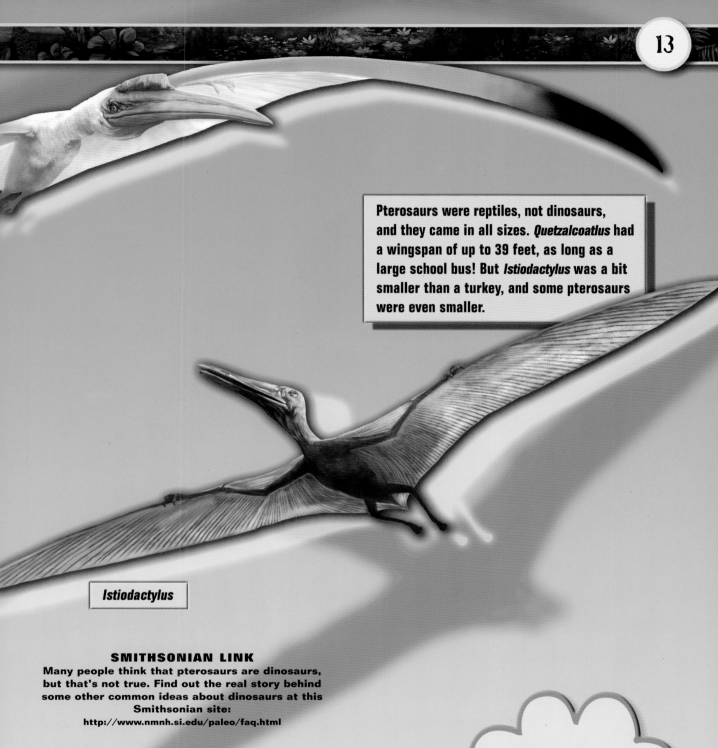

Pterosaurs were reptiles, not dinosaurs, and they came in all sizes. *Quetzalcoatlus* had a wingspan of up to 39 feet, as long as a large school bus! But *Istiodactylus* was a bit smaller than a turkey, and some pterosaurs were even smaller.

Istiodactylus

SMITHSONIAN LINK
Many people think that pterosaurs are dinosaurs, but that's not true. Find out the real story behind some other common ideas about dinosaurs at this Smithsonian site:
http://www.nmnh.si.edu/paleo/faq.html

Istiodactylus:
ISS-tee-oh-DAK-till-us

Quetzalcoatlus:
ket-sul-KWAT-luss

Even though the *Ophthalmosaurus* looked like a dolphin, it was really a reptile that had to come to the surface for air.

Could dinosaurs swim?

Dinosaurs could probably swim if they had to. But they spent most of their lives on solid ground. Other animals ruled the rivers, lakes, and oceans. There were sharks and crocodiles, fish and turtles. And there were other water animals, too, ones that we will never see today.

Ichthyosaurs probably hunted fish and squid. *Ophthalmosaurus,* an ichthyosaur, had larger eyes for its size than any other animal. Maybe such big eyes helped it to see when it dived to hunt in deep, dark water.

Ichthyosaurs were aquatic animals. They spent their lives in water.

No dinosaurs were aquatic.

ichthyosaur:
ICK-thee-uh-sore

Ophthalmosaurus:
of-THAL-mo-SORE-us

Seismosaurus, meaning "earth-shaking lizard," was a giant sauropod that lived during the Jurassic period.

How big were dinosaurs?

One of the longest dinosaurs we know about was *Seismosaurus*. It was longer than a basketball court. Its neck was so long that it probably couldn't raise its head very high. If it did, its heart would not have been able to pump hard enough to get blood all the way up to its brain!

Eoraptor:
EE-oh-RAP-tor

Microraptor:
MY-crow-RAP-tor

Seismosaurus:
size-muh-SORE-us

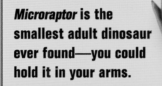

Microraptor is the smallest adult dinosaur ever found—you could hold it in your arms.

Were all dinosaurs big?

Not all of them. *Eoraptor*, an early dinosaur, was about 3 feet long—as big as a medium-sized dog. *Microraptor* was the size of a crow and had feathers on its arms and legs. It may have lived in trees.

Dinosaurs came in many sizes. Because it's easier for paleontologists to find giant bones than small ones, we know most about the biggest dinosaurs.

SMITHSONIAN LINK
Why did some dinosaurs grow so big? Find out the answer
to that question and many others about dinosaurs at:
http://www.nmnh.si.edu/paleo/dinosaurs/info/faq/faq_8.html

What did dinosaurs eat?

With its powerful jaws, a *T. rex* could bite harder than a crocodile or a great white shark.

Whether they were huge like *Seismosaurus* or tiny like *Microraptor*, all dinosaurs needed food, just as all animals do today.

Most dinosaurs, such as *Seismosaurus*, were plant eaters. Their teeth had different shapes depending on what they ate. Some had broad, flat teeth for grinding, and others had leaf-shaped teeth for cutting and slicing.

Other dinosaurs, such as *Tyrannosaurus rex*, were meat eaters. Their teeth were long and sharp, like knives. They bit off chunks of flesh from other animals but couldn't chew them. Instead they swallowed the pieces whole. *Coelophysis* was another meat eater. In its stomach, scientists have found fossilized bones from small reptiles, fish, and baby *Coelophysis*!

Coelophysis:
SEE-low-FIE-sis

Tyrannosaurus rex:
tuh-ran-uh-SORE-us RECKS

Some dinosaurs probably lived alone most of their lives, staying with another of their kind only long enough to mate. Some animals such as tigers and sharks live like this today.

Other present-day animals (such as wolves, fish, and horses) live in groups. Maybe some dinosaurs did, too. Plant eaters, such as hadrosaurs, may have lived together. *Tyrannosaurus rex* might have found it easy to have a lone hadrosaur for dinner.

Living in a group was safer.

Perhaps one hadrosaur kept watch for danger while the rest grazed on leaves or grasses. Or maybe hadrosaurs fought together to keep a meat eater from getting near their young.

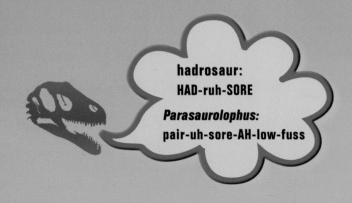

hadrosaur:
HAD-ruh-SORE

Parasaurolophus:
pair-uh-sore-AH-low-fuss

Did dinosaurs live alone?

Parasaurolophus had a long, hollow bone inside the crest on its head. Perhaps it could use this crest to make a honking noise to signal others in its herd.

What were dinosaur babies like?

Maiasaura, meaning "good mother lizard," protected her nest against predators and weather.

Dinosaur babies hatched out of eggs. Some survived on their own and never saw their parents. Others were weak and helpless. Their parents protected and fed them until they could live on their own.

Some dinosaurs sat on their eggs to keep them safe and warm, just as chickens do today. Scientists have found fossils of *Oviraptor* that were killed by sandstorms or dune slides while sitting on their nests. Perhaps they would not abandon their eggs even to save their lives.

Large dinosaurs such as *Maiasaura* probably covered their nests with leaves and plants to keep the eggs warm.

Some dinosaur eggs could be as long as 16 inches—that's bigger than a whole carton of eggs in your grocery store.

Maiasaura:
MY-uh-SORE-uh

Oviraptor:
OH-vih-RAP-tor

A 6,000-pound *Maiasaura* mother could never have sat on her eggs—she would have crushed them to bits!

How smart were dinosaurs?

A fossil can't tell us how a dinosaur thought. But it can tell us how big a dinosaur's brain was. *Apatosaurus* had a giant body 100,000 times the size of its tiny brain! It was probably not much smarter than a crocodile.

Other dinosaurs had bigger brains. *Troodon*, a meat-eating dinosaur, had the largest brain for its body size. Maybe *Troodon*'s big brain helped it figure out how to catch animals to eat.

Was a dinosaur as smart as a dog? A monkey? A mouse? We can't say for sure. But we know that dinosaurs lived on Earth for millions of years. They were smart enough to make the choices that let them survive.

To survive, an animal needs to find food and keep from being eaten by something else. Dinosaurs solved these problems in different ways.

Meat eaters such as *Troodon* needed big brains to help them hunt down their prey.

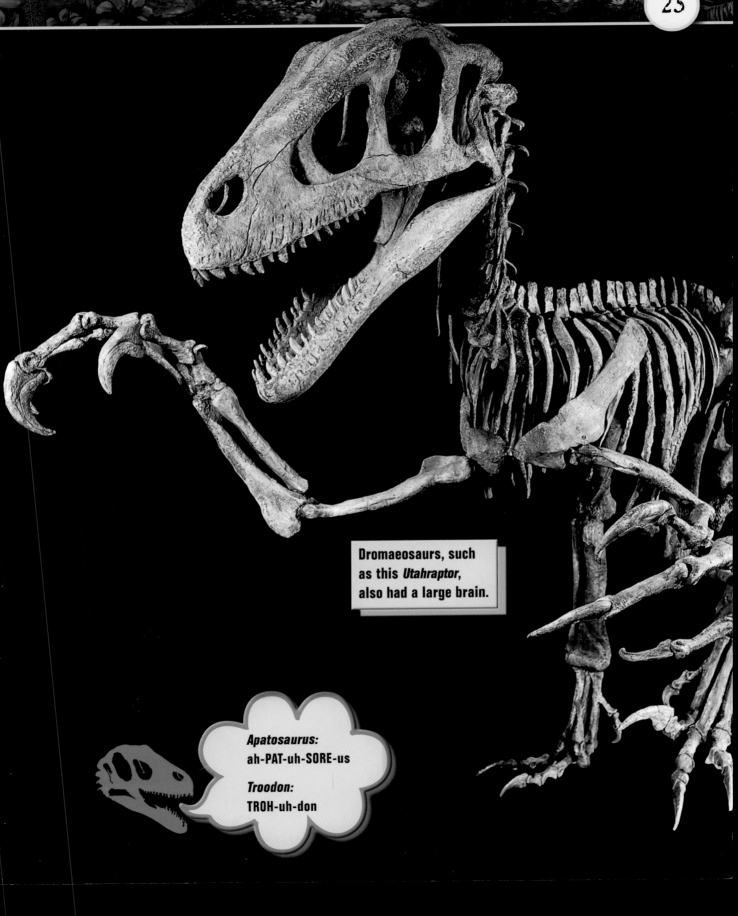

Dromaeosaurs, such as this *Utahraptor*, also had a large brain.

Apatosaurus:
ah-PAT-uh-SORE-us

Troodon:
TROH-uh-don

What were a *Tyrannosaurus rex's* teeth for?

Not only did *T. rex* have deadly teeth, it could also see and smell very well. Its keen senses helped it find food.

SMITHSONIAN LINK
See *T. rex* and other dinosaurs of the Cretaceous period at this Smithsonian site:
http://www.nmnh.si.edu/paleo/dino/kperiod.htm

Tyrannosaurus rex, or *T. rex*, had teeth the size of bananas, about fifty of them. Those teeth could slice off a mouthful of meat the size of a wolf.

With *T. rex*'s sharp teeth and powerful jaw, most people think it must have been a deadly hunter. But a few scientists wonder if *T. rex* hunted at all. They think it might have been a **scavenger**, using its teeth to cut up animals that had already died. Or maybe it did both, killing when it could and eating dead meat if that was all it could find.

Tyrannosaurus rex was one kind of tyrannosaur. All tyrannosaurs had a long, stiff tail, powerful back legs, and little arms. In fact, *T. rex*'s arms were too short to get food to its mouth. What did it use them for?

Maybe someday we'll find out.

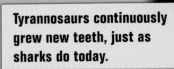

Tyrannosaurs continuously grew new teeth, just as sharks do today.

What were a Velociraptor's claws for?

A *Velociraptor* had a strong, curved claw on the second toe of each back foot. How did it keep its claws from rubbing against the ground and getting dull? It held its toe up to keep the claw away from the ground. That way it stayed sharp.

A *Velociraptor* used its claws to bring down animals to eat.

Perhaps it slashed at its **prey**, opening up bleeding wounds to weaken the other animal. Or perhaps it used its claws like spikes, digging them into a bigger animal's skin so it could climb up its side, biting and clawing as it went. Either way, *Velociraptor* must have been a deadly hunter.

Velociraptor: veh-LOSS-ih-RAP-tor

New evidence from fossils indicates that the *Velociraptor* may have actually had feathers.

Velociraptor was about 4 feet tall. With its sharp claws, it didn't need to be huge to be fierce.

Standing more than 50 feet, *Sauroposeidon* is the tallest dinosaur ever discovered.

What was a Sauroposeidon's neck for?

Sauroposeidon had a neck eight times longer than a giraffe's. Teeth and claws helped meat eaters get food. *Sauroposeidon* was a plant eater, and its neck helped it find food. It could have stretched out its neck to eat plants in a wide area without moving its heavy feet.

Sauroposeidon also had strong, clawed feet and a long tail. It probably used these to protect itself against **predators** eager for a huge meal.

Sauroposeidon was one of the biggest animals that ever lived on land. It needed to eat a lot, and that long neck made it easier.

Sauroposeidon:
SORE-uh-po-sie-don

The pattern of the plates and spikes was different for each species of stegosaur. Some even had spikes on their shoulders.

SMITHSONIAN LINK
The *Stegosaurus* is famous for its spiked tail. View the Smithsonian FossiLab slide show of how a model is made from a *Stegosaurus* fossil:
http://www.nmnh.si.edu/paleo/dinosaurs/info/new/070103.html

What was a Stegosaurus's tail for?

A *Stegosaurus* couldn't run fast, but it didn't need to. On the end of its strong tail it had sharp spikes as long as your arm.

It could **swing its tail** to keep enemies away.

Other dinosaurs had tough plates, spikes, or horns to protect themselves. But some prey animals did not have defenses such as these. How did they keep themselves safe? Perhaps they ran away from predators or protected themselves by living in groups.

Stegosaurus:
ste-guh-SORE-us

Did dinosaurs have feathers?

For a long time people thought that birds were the only animals with feathers. But now we know that some dinosaurs, such as *Caudipteryx*, had feathers, too.

Caudipteryx could not have used its feathers to fly—they didn't make a big enough wing.

Caudipteryx:
caw-DIP-ter-icks

What were feathers good for if they didn't let a dinosaur fly?

A peacock's tail does not help it fly. It uses its beautiful tail feathers to attract a mate. Maybe *Caudipteryx* did the same. A kiwi is another bird that can't fly. Its brown, hairy feathers keep it warm. Maybe *Caudipteryx* used feathers to stay warm in cold weather.

Caudipteryx was about the size of a chicken. It was the first dinosaur with feathers to be discovered.

What happened to all the dinosaurs?

You will never see a *T. rex* lurking in your backyard or a *Triceratops* grazing on plants in the park. These dinosaurs died out about 65 million years ago.

Around the time many dinosaurs became **extinct**, a huge rock from space struck Earth. The **asteroid** caused earthquakes, fires, tidal waves, and hurricanes. Even worse, it kicked up clouds of dust that blocked the sun. Plants could not grow. The dinosaurs that ate plants died. Without the plant eaters, meat eaters had no

food either. They starved to death.

Not everyone thinks that the asteroid alone was enough to kill off so many dinosaurs. There might have been other causes, such as a big change in the weather or many volcanoes erupting around the same time. We don't know exactly what happened, but we know it was a huge disaster.

SMITHSONIAN LINK
New evidence suggests proof of an asteroid hitting Earth around the time of the dinosaurs' extinction:
http://www.nmnh.si.edu/paleo/blast/index.html

Did any dinosaurs survive?

Look out your window. Do you see a robin hunting for a worm or a blue jay building a nest? Then you have seen an animal that many scientists think is related to dinosaurs.

A robin doesn't look very much like a *Tyrannosaurus rex*. But when scientists look at the skeletons of birds and dinosaurs, they find that the bones are very much alike. And we know today that some dinosaurs had feathers like birds.

Birds **evolved** sometime during the Jurassic period from small predatory dinosaurs. How did this happen? Each baby dinosaur that hatched was a tiny bit different from its parents. Over millions of years, dinosaurs evolved. Today, most scientists believe that birds are **descendants** of the dinosaurs.

Most experts now agree that birds, such as this blue jay, are direct descendants of dinosaurs.

While most birds do not look like dinosaurs, their bone structures are very similar.

These fossilized footprints are in Colorado, where a sauropod like *Apatosaurus* walked long ago.

Do we know everything about dinosaurs?

Have we found out all there is to know? Not at all! Scientists keep working on new mysteries. Maybe soon they'll learn the answer to a hard question: Were dinosaurs **warm-blooded** like mammals and birds or **cold-blooded** like reptiles? Or were they something in between?

Fossilized footprints sometimes hint at another dinosaur mystery. At times scientists find footprints that could not have been made by any dinosaur we know about. They can study the tracks and come up with some ideas about what kind of dinosaur walked over muddy ground millions of years ago. But they can't know for sure what that dinosaur was like—until the day a paleontologist digs up a new fossil and discovers a new kind of dinosaur.

Maybe that paleontologist will be YOU.

SMITHSONIAN LINK
Studying dinosaur tracks can give you the size and shape and number of toes. To get more information on how tracking footprints works, check out this site:
http://paleo.cc/paluxy/ovrdino.htm

This time line shows when each of the animals mentioned in *Extreme Dinosaurs* was alive.

MESOZOIC ERA
(251–65 million years ago)

TRIASSIC PERIOD
(251–200 million years ago)

cockroaches • *Coelophysis* • crocodiles • *Eoraptor*
pterosaurs • sharks • turtles

JURASSIC PERIOD
(200–146 million years ago)

Allosaurus • *Apatosaurus* • birds • cockroaches
lizards • mammals • *Ophthalmosaurus* • pterosaurs
Stegosaurus • turtles

CRETACEOUS PERIOD
(146–65 million years ago)

birds • *Caudipteryx* • cockroaches • crocodiles • fish
Maiasaura • mammals • *Microraptor* • *Oviraptor*
salamanders • *Sauroposeidon* • sharks • *Troodon*

Cretaceous: cri-TAY-shus
Jurassic: joo-RAS-ick
Mesozoic: meh-zuh-ZOH-ick
Triassic: try-AS-ick

Quetzalcoatlus

fish • frogs • ichthyosaurs • mammals

Stegosaurus

**crocodiles • fish • frogs • ichthyosaurs
salamanders • *Seismosaurus* • sharks**

Sauroposeidon

**frogs • ichthyosaurs • *Istiodactylus* • lizards
Parasaurolophus • pterosaurs • *Quetzalcoatlus*
turtles • *Tyrannosaurus rex* • *Utahraptor* • *Velociraptor***

SMITHSONIAN LINK
Dinosaurs lived millions of years ago. To measure such huge amounts of
time, scientists use something called "geologic time." To see when dinosaurs
and other animals (including humans) first appeared on Earth, visit
http://www.nmnh.si.edu/paleo/dino/timescal.htm

Meet the Paleontologist

Dr. Matthew Carrano
CURATOR
NATIONAL MUSEUM OF NATURAL HISTORY

Why did you become a scientist?

I became a scientist because I was fascinated by paleontology and by trying to understand *why* things happened. I found that the way science asks questions about the world was very interesting and satisfying to me.

What incident or person from your childhood influenced your decision?

I read a dinosaur book for the first time when I was in second grade, and I immediately decided to become a paleontologist. I was influenced by the *Age of Reptiles* mural in the Peabody Museum, near where I grew up.

How can kids get interested in your field?

The best way to get interested is by reading books and visiting museums. Sometimes it's possible to visit a real dig site, too.

Where do you do your research?

I spend part of every day doing research in the museum, both in the library and in the fossil collections. I also spend a few weeks every year out in the field looking for fossils.

What are the most important qualities for an expert in your field?

The best paleontologists love to ask questions and are good at thinking about ways to solve complicated problems. As a scientist, you have to get used to arguing over things with your colleagues and to being wrong a lot of the time.

Where have you traveled for your job?

I do fieldwork, looking for new fossils, and have been to Madagascar and Chile and all across the American West.

What is the biggest recent discovery in your field?

Probably the biggest recent news has been the discovery of dinosaurs with feathers and featherlike structures. Aside from strengthening the bird-dinosaur link, finding feathers on nonflying dinosaurs shows that feathers must have evolved before flight.

Is there something in your field you wish was studied more?

Sort of; there are things I wish were studied less. I think paleontologists spend too much time studying predatory dinosaurs, such as *Tyrannosaurus rex* and *Velociraptor*. We don't spend enough time on the other kinds of dinosaurs, and so we don't understand them as well as we should.

What do you like most about your job?

Most of all, I love that I get to work with real fossils every single day.

What was the most exciting discovery you ever made?

So far, the most exciting thing has been part of a skull of the predator dinosaur *Majungasaurus*, when I was on a field expedition in Madagascar. It was thrilling to brush the dirt away and see a row of sharp teeth gleaming in the sun.

Glossary

asteroid—A piece of rock from space. Asteroids that fall into Earth's atmosphere become meteors. If they strike the ground, they are called meteorites.

cold-blooded—Does not keep a steady body temperature. Cold-blooded animals rely on activity or outside sources (such as sun or shade) to warm up or cool down.

descendant—A person or animal that is related to someone or something that lived before. You are a descendant of your parents and grandparents.

evolve—To develop or change over time. Animals evolve because each baby is a little bit different from its parents. If the difference helps the baby survive, grow up, and have babies of its own, it will be passed down. Over millions of years, one kind of animal can evolve into another. Scientists think that some dinosaurs evolved into birds.

extinct—Not existing on Earth anymore. An animal is extinct when the last one of that kind of animal has died.

fossil—Any evidence of past life. A piece of an animal's body, a plant, or a trace of an animal (such as a footprint) that has been preserved in stone.

ice cap—A thick sheet of ice that covers the land around the North and South Poles of the Earth.

mammal—A warm-blooded animal that gives birth to its babies (instead of laying eggs) and feeds them milk. Most mammals are covered with fur.

mineral—A natural, solid substance that is not alive. Diamond, emerald, gold, graphite (the lead in your pencil), iron, and quartz are all minerals.

paleontologist—A scientist who studies ancient life, including dinosaurs, by examining fossils.

predator—An animal that hunts other animals to eat them.

prey—An animal that is hunted.

reptile—Scaly, land-living animals, including lizards, snakes, turtles, crocodiles, and dinosaurs.

scavenger—An animal that feeds on dead animals.

warm-blooded—Keeps a steady body temperature. Warm-blooded animals make their own warmth inside their bodies, whether the air around them is hot or cool.

More to See and Read

Websites

There are links to many wonderful web pages in this book.
But the web is constantly growing and changing, so we cannot
guarantee that the sites we recommend will be available.
If the site you want is no longer there, you can always
find your way to plenty of information about
dinosaurs and a great learning experience
through the main Smithsonian website:
www.si.edu.

Find frequently asked questions and answers about dinosaurs at this Smithsonian
website: http://www.nmnh.si.edu/paleo/dinosaurs/info/faq/main.html

Visiting a museum and seeing dinosaur fossils up close is one of the best ways to learn
more about them. To find out about the dinosaur exhibits at the Smithsonian National
Museum of Natural History, visit: http://www.nmnh.si.edu/paleo/dino/index.html

And to find a dinosaur museum near where you live, try:
http://www.nmnh.si.edu/paleo/dinosaurs/collection/where/main.html

To learn more about many kinds of dinosaurs and to search for the type of dinosaur you want to
investigate, visit: http://www.dinosauria.com

What were the biggest, fastest, slowest, smartest dinosaurs? Try this website to find out:
http://www.factmonster.com/ipka/a0770763.html

To see movies of animated dinosaurs, try this site:
http://dsc.discovery.com/convergence/dinos/video/video.html

To find out about a fossil-gathering expedition and see fossils of dinosaur eggs and embryos
(unhatched babies), visit: http://www.amnh.org/exhibitions/expeditions/dinosaur/patagonia

Suggested Reading

The Day the Dinosaurs Died by Charlotte
Lewis Brown, illustrated by Phil Wilson

Dinosaurs by Rachel Firth, illustrated by
Franco Tempesta

Extreme Dinosaurs by Luis V. Rey

*New Dinos: The Latest Finds! The Coolest
Dinosaur Discoveries!* by Shelley Tanaka,
illustrated by Alan Barnard

Did Dinosaurs Have Feathers? by Kathleen
Weidner Zoehfeld, illustrated by Lucia
Washburn

*Dinosaur Parents, Dinosaur Young: Uncovering
the Mystery of Dinosaur Families* by Kathleen
Weidner Zoehfeld

Index